Dedication

I wrote this in memory of Michael McNeil and Dawn Greene. My heart and mind were not ready to face your tragedies. I am no longer angry, only wishing that you were here daily.

-Tai

Table of contents

Introduction

1. Session one
2. Session Two
3. Session Three
4. Session Four

Introduction

In elementary school I was homeless, in middle school I was suicidal, in high school I was drowning, and, in my mind, it could not get any darker. "It's dark" is a phrase that I use to describe the state of my mental health when I feel like my depression is taking over. Believe it or not there are more children in elementary school that are homeless, do not know where their next meal is coming from or being abused verbally, physically, and mentally. Those children are capable of being depressed; depression does not have an age range. My first day of seventh grade I literally got dressed in the dark after bathing with cold water because we did not have electricity. I had the hardest struggle of trying to maintain an appearance that I was "okay" like every other student, make new friends, keep up my grades and leave the darkness of what is going at home, at home. When I was 17, I ran away, because I knew that was the only way I could save myself. This book is not just to give a back story of my life, but to speak my truth and my truth alone. Of course, there are two sides of every story and this is mine. Every trial that I faced made me stronger. As cliché as that may sound. To everyone facing these battles or trying to face battles of the past, I hope this helps. The title of this is silent black screams because I suffered in silence, but my silence was my cry. Black is the absence of light that I thought I would not see. Screaming is what I felt like I was doing mentally because I would not speak of the pain. Throughout this book there are a few pages dedicated to exercises that I hope you take the time to complete.

2:07 p.m. September, 2019

I'm just leaving work and as I'm exiting the base, I'm calling Thrive Works Counseling to begin working with a therapist. The phone rings and the receptionist goes over a series of questions and finally reached the most important one, why do you think you need a counselor?

WHY?

"I need a counselor because there is a war inside myself that I am losing. I do not know how to control my thoughts, I do not know how to let the past go, I do not know how to break the cycle of my random depressive episodes and most importantly, I do not know how to stop isolating myself when all of these issues begin to take over." She proceeded to schedule the initial consultation appointment and a week later I was sitting in front of an African American woman, hesitant to pour my heart out when answering these questions about my upbringing, my relationships, my friends, my emotions, and my darkness, because let's be honest, I don't really know how to be vulnerable.

Questions:

1. Are you in school?
2. Did you have an easy childhood? If not, explain.
3. Are you close to your family? Who do you consider family?
4. What boundaries do you have with your family?
5. Who are you closest to?
6. Do you have friends? If so, who are they?

7. Are you single?

8. What is your sexual orientation?

9. What relationships left the greatest mark on your heart?

10. Why are you here? What are you expecting to gain from this experience?

11. What health conditions do you have?

12. Do you have thoughts of harming yourself?

By the time our session concluded, I was anxious to see her again. She was easy to talk to, relatable, she spoke to me in my language and I knew I needed a counselor that I could trust and be comfortable with.

1ˢᵗ Session

I pulled into the parking lot early, my mind was going 120mph wondering what today would be like. Would this session drag up unwanted and suppressed feelings or would we just scratch the surface? I signed in, paid my copay, and sat down.

Tatyaniah? She spoke.

Yes? I replied.

Hey, you can come back now. You look like you're fresh off work she said.

We went into her office, I sat in the single seat in the corner and she looked at me and said "Are you comfortable there?" I looked around and said "yes, should I sit somewhere else?" She replied "it's whatever you're comfortable with."

What would you like to start with today? She asked.

Boundaries. I said.

What about them? Who do you need to set boundaries with? She asked.

Everyone. I said

Elaborate please she requested.

I go above and beyond for people and I feel like it's not appreciated or reciprocated. I feel as if there are too many people around me that are not genuine. I'm constantly giving and they're constantly taking and it's draining me. I need to put a cap on it. I replied.

Tatyaniah. Actually, would you prefer I call you something different? She asked.

Tatyaniah is fine. I said.

Tatyaniah you're being vague. Break it down for me. She said.

Ok so I go above and beyond for my siblings no matter what they ask for I make it happen. Would a "thank you" be too much to ask for? I do what I do because I don't want them to feel like they're missing something or can't have something because I felt that way growing up even though my mom did everything she could. I help my mom out because I'm supposed to make sure they're all ok. If my friends/ people, I'm close to need anything I'm there; because you're supposed to show up for your friends and support them. In romantic relationships I'm giving as much as I can in all areas, and it doesn't seem to be enough. I expressed.

Who's showing up for you the way you feel like you show up for them? She asked.

I stared.

Silence

No one. I responded.

So why are you doing so much? She asked.

I'm supposed to. I am the person I want other people to be for me. I said.

Who made that your job? She asked.

Me? I said puzzled.

Right. You are not obligated to be a bank or second parent. It is not your job to pour into people or situations that are leaving you empty. She explained.

Silence

You must learn how to say no with no explanation. No matter what someone has or has not done for or to you. You probably feel resentment towards them, and they don't even know it. Am I right? She continued.

Yes. I replied.

So why won't you speak up and hold them accountable? She asked.

I'm thinking to myself; I really don't know.

To keep the peace. I replied.

When you avoid speaking up to avoid conflict and keep the peace on the outside, you begin to create a war inside yourself with the feelings that you are harboring. She said.

You are absolutely right. I stated.

Now, I am not saying that your feelings are always right. You must put fact over feeling when trying to place things into perspective in any situation. Yes, you are entitled to feel any way you please, those are your feelings; but own them. Nobody is making you feel that way she said.

What do you mean? I asked.

For example…. Let's say I say told someone something about you and the comment made its way back to you and it pisses you off, right? You should be able to come to me and say "Shay I didn't like that you were repeating things that I told you in confidence, I felt betrayed." And not "you hurt me when…" Do you see the difference?

Ok, I get it. I said.

Fact

Feeling

Now let's talk about relationships she said.

I rolled my eyes.

She laughed and said, "girl it can't be that bad."

I laughed and said "sis, you not ready for me."

She laughed.

I said "ok so, my last relationship literally just ended and what started off great didn't take long to take a turn for the worst and I ignored all the red flags. She was controlling, manipulative, I noticed how she would try to isolate me from my family simply because she was not close to hers and didn't really want a relationship with them. She wanted me to fill the void of her mother, father, sister, brother etc. all while I had to manage school, work, my own mental health, and everything else and I could not be everything for her.

That is correct. She said.

I continued with saying that I really loved her undoubtedly, I wanted to help her, I really did, and I tried but she was not ready to face it. I know that you cannot help someone who does not want to help themselves. But I would be lying if I said that I loved her nearly as much as I loved him though and she could feel that.

Who is he? She asked.

He and I started dating in November of 2012. We have known each other since we were in the 3rd grade. He is my best friend, well was. But throughout our relationship he cheated more than enough, and I got tired and I left. He is an amazing person, a good friend, to this day if I ever need him I know he is going to come, but as a faithful boyfriend he sucks in that aspect. I said.

What if the timing wasn't right? She said I am not making excuses for him, but I will say men tend to explore in their younger years and maybe he wasn't as mature as you at that time. Are you willing to try again with him? She asked.

We broke up in 2017 and I left it there. I love him, but not enough to keep letting him hurt me. At some point I had to love me more. I said.

But y'all have been apart for a few years, people can change and grow. That version of him that you have in your head may no longer exist. She then asked has he tried to pursue you after the breakup. She said.

He never stopped I said, he even got our date tattooed on his leg with the date of the last child we lost together. I responded.

Sounds like a guy that may have learned his lesson to me, but I can't speak for him. She said.

Silence

Why couldn't you love her as much as you loved him? She asked

I am not sure, maybe because she wasn't him and I saw so much of him in her. Literally their birthdays are one day apart. I know she is not him though. I responded.

How much do you love him? She asked

He is literally my heartbeat walking the earth. I am 100% myself and open with him, well I was. I said.

You never 100% separated yourself from him and that is another reason why you and her couldn't work. Yes, she had her issues, but you contributed to her insecurities when it came to you and him. She stated.

I stopped talking to him for the sake of our relationship and that hurt him, but I wanted to be with her. I said.

Sometimes we need to take breaks from people when we are growing in different directions and they reconvene later in life. We are human, we all make mistakes, and we should all learn from them. I would never tell you what to do, I am simply stating that people change and if you decided to try again that is completely up to you and him. You do not owe anyone an explanation about what happens between you and him, and it's honestly better to not vent to friends or family about certain things because they become too involved. She explained.

A MOUTHFUL!

I stared.

Have you forgiven him? She asked.

NO! I proclaimed.

Oh, I can tell. She said.

We both laughed.

You must forgive him Tatyaniah, y'all were teenagers and that is so common at that age although it causes damage. You were both trying to figure out who y'all were. You wanted children, marriage, and everything by 25; meanwhile he was enjoying life. Y'all were on two different ends of the spectrum and you cannot fault him for that. He is entitled to live the way he wants, minus cheating. He was entitled to enjoy his youth. You must forgive him and let go of the pain. She spoke.

How? I asked.

Acknowledge and accept it first. Do not continue to suppress feelings that you do not have to hold onto, you are carrying a burden that you need to let go. You cannot move past it if you do not heal. LET IT GO! She said. I'm going to give you homework she added. Here is a list of questions that I want you to answer truthfully and we're going to discuss them next week.

Is our hour up? I asked anxiously.

No, we have about 25 minutes left, let's talk about these friendships. She said.

What about them. I said.

Who are they and how do you feel about them? She said.

My very first best friend lives in Norfolk, VA. We meet in 7th grade; we were actually bitchy towards each other and somehow, we still ended up being best friends. We have been through our ups and downs and the only issue I have now is that I feel like I travel to see her more than she sees me, and I know we are in different places in life, but it still bothers me. I know that can be fixed though.

And who else she said?

The second one lives here in Columbia, sc. That's my dawg for real! We honestly do not fight, we have petty disagreements and we both say how we feel and we're done with it. I can be honest and open with her 110% and there is never any judgement on either end. We genuinely support each other and are there. Well I guess she is the person that shows up for me in that way. No matter what, she's there. She is actually the first person to genuinely tell me that I needed to see someone about my mental health. I said.

Is this the healthiest relationship you feel that you've ever had? She said.

Yes. I responded.

How did you meet her? She asked.

At work back in 2014, we instantly clicked, and it's been a vibe ever since.

Did y'all ever cross that line? She asked.

Yes, but that was years ago, and we completely do not even bring that up or act any way regarding it. We are around each other's significant others and everything. I said.

Did your girlfriend know that? She asked.

Yes, I did not lie to her about anything from my past. I said.

Ok anyone else? Said.

Yes, I have another friend that live in Hampton, VA. I literally enjoy the way we can talk about anything and enjoy each other even if we have not seen or spoken to each other in a while. There is a side of me that she understands that others don't. And she's crazy I said, I love it.

Lastly, there is one from Atlanta and sometimes I feel like our friendship is one sided but I know financially she is going through things so I can't be mad. But I feel like it's been this way since I met her. I don't know. But she is my friend, I genuinely enjoy her company and everything it's just a feeling about that one aspect.

Why does everyone feel so comfortable asking you for money? Why do they think you have so much money? She asked.

Honestly, I think it is partly because people feel that anyone in the military must have money, but they do not know what happens behind the scenes. I have a savings account now that I will not touch no matter what, I do not know what is in it. But that is for later in life. I said.

Why is saving that money so important to you? She asked.

Because I know what it is like to be homeless. I said.

Silence

We wrapped up our session and I walked out feeling a bit lighter than when I went in. My cousin called and asked how it was and I said great. She asked if I thought it would actually help and I said yes. This isn't my first time, only my first time going on my own.

Exercises

I would like for you to complete these exercises. You do not have to share with anyone, and I am not a counselor or therapist. These exercises simply helped me and maybe they can help you as well. Take your time and answer them truthfully, burn it when you are done if it will make things easier.

WHAT DO YOU NEED?

1. What do you think you deserve or need just by being human alone? Both physically and emotionally?

2. What is standing in the way of you reaching these needs?

3. Identify 3 or more times that you actually stepped outside of your comfort zone to meet these needs.

4. What are your clues that someone is taking advantage of you?

What's your pleasure?

1. What activities do you enjoy that are relaxing to you?

2. What are a few physical pleasures that make you feel good?

3. Whose company do you genuinely enjoy?

4. What material items boost your confidence?

Define the relationship!

List the roles that you expect the people to fill in your life and explain your expectations of them and why (lover, mother, teacher, kids or employer).

1. *Do you think these expectations can be reasonably met?*

2. *Are you willing to share this with these people?*

3. *What does this say about your relationship with them?*

2nd Session

3:53 P.M October 2019

All week I have been saying in my head that I cannot wait to tell my therapist about every inconvenience that has occurred in my life. After work I drove to Columbia, took a deep breath in the parking lot, walked in paid my copay and waited.

Ms. Tatyaniah? She spoke.

I stood up and said hey and we walked to her office.

How are you feeling today? She asked.

Good. I responded.

Did you bring your homework? She asked.

Of course. I responded.

I handed her my papers, and my anxiety was on the rise.

She reviewed them, asked me why I felt that way about a few of them, took some notes and we moved on.

What's on your mind today? She asked.

I saw my ex-girlfriend at work, and she is so persistent on being the person I needed her to be now and not when I wanted it. It's all weird to me because sis, you are already dating someone new that you met when you were away at an Army school. She asked me would I agree to be in a poly relationship and that girl can kiss my entire ass for real. I do not want her friendship or poly relationship. I said.

Did you tell her that? She asked.

Yes, and she said I really do not want to lose either of you, so I told her it's cool because I was going to choose for her. I replied.

Why don't you want to be at least friends with her? She asked.

Because I have seen the type of friend, she is to everyone else and why would I ever want that? Plus, my feelings for her are not completely gone and it would hurt me more, I am trying to heal and move on, not hold on. I spoke.

Are you sure? She asked.

AS FUCK! I spoke.

Ok, so did we use anything we learned in our last session?

Yes, I have started saying no with no explanation and spending more money on me. I spoke.

And how is that going? She asked.

I feel good.

Are we spending frivolously? She asked.

I do have a bad habit of going on shopping sprees to get myself out of bad mood and I do not look at price tags, because if I want it, I am going to get it. And that is a bad habit that I picked up from her and I need to break it. I spoke.

Get whatever you want but be smart about it. She spoke.

Oh wait, did you talk to him? She added.

Yes, the day I left here I called him and said I was coming over to have a conversation and I did. We discussed our past issues and current for 100th time and he apologized just as he has 1 million times before. He knows that I am working on forgiving him and I also told him that if there is ever a chance in hell of us getting back together, we have to rebuild a friendship, but one even stronger than before. I know he does not want to be my friend, but he accepted anyway. I know it hurts him to see me moving the way I am now because all he wants is for us to fix things, but I cannot. Not right now. I told her.

It is a start. I am going to ask you for random updates about you and him, but I do hope that the two of you stick with it because I am sure you both have a lot of love for each other. Remember that people can change, but on their time, not yours. She stated.

Understood. I replied.

Other than boundaries, what are some things you need to work on? She asked.

Patience for sure, that is something I lack tremendously, stubbornness, because once I am set in my ways, that is it. Overthinking is another one of my biggest challenges because I can literally think myself into a bad mood and miscarriages because I need to heal. Oh, and isolation. I am hurting someone close to me every time I do that. I spoke.

Why do you isolate? She asked.

Because my misery does not like company. I do not like company. I stated.

So, because you are sad or in a bad mood that means you cannot talk to or be around anyone for however long? She asked. Tell me what happens when you are isolating and who you are hurting.

I ignore phone calls, text messages, watch television, eat maybe once a day, go to work, and back home and never leave again until it's time for work. I do that for weeks before it gets better. I am hurting my cousin because she and I are so close and we talk throughout the day everyday so when I stop answering and responding to her, she told me she does not like it, but I do answer eventually even if its short and she does not like it. I did finally tell her that I was not in a good place recently and I was taking a step back to get myself together and I know she did not like it, but she understood. I responded.

It is unhealthy. She stated.

Sis, that why I came here, I know that. I need help. I spoke.

What do you say to people when they ask how you are feeling during this time? She asked.

It's dark! I spoke.

And what does that mean to you? She inquired.

My depression is taking over and I might not know why, and I do not know for how long, but I am trying. I spoke.

Let's try to force ourselves to do a few things when its dark she says.

1. Go outside, I do not care if it is just to sit in the car with the windows down, you need to get some fresh air and sunlight outside of the house.
2. Dance, play loud music, run, go to the gym or whatever is going to get you active, but MOVE!
3. Work on something that brings you joy, like take another baking class or something.
4. Meditate

5. Whenever something negative is bothering you, give yourself 7 minutes to feel it and take 5 deep breaths and keep going on about your day. You cannot sit in that dark place and let it take over. Did you know that we as humans are truly only mad for a few seconds, but we allow the issue to linger on and that is why we remain upset for so long. Tatyaniah, LET GO!

6. Cry. If you need to let it out, let it out. Crying does not make you weak and you must start allowing yourself to truly feel these feelings so that you can move on from them. Suppression is never going to work.

She went on to email me a list to remind me.

I am going to try it. I said.

Honestly, it helped me. Meditating and stretching was my go-to. I use the oak app which is amazing, and it sends out real life quotes every day at 8:35 p.m. My favorite quote is "the root of all suffering is attachment."

Are you sexually active? She asked.

Well, that escalated quickly. I said.

With whom? Him and her? She asked.

No, with him and someone else. When I randomly miss him and want sex with him then I hit him up and I know he is never going to say no and when I simply text him, we link up, we have sex and then I go. I never have sex with him and the other at the same time and I get tested every three months and I am honest with both. I responded.

They are ok with it? She asked.

They do not have to be. They can leave or say no whenever they want. I have toys that can get the job done. I said.

She laughed and said is that enough for you?

Yes. I set these terms. I do not want any emotional attachments right now. The other guy is great though, we are friends, we chill, he gives the most levelheaded advice, he tutored me, we he tried at least I said as I chuckled. We know we like each other, but we leave it alone and we do not talk every day. I get what I want and go without all the relationship drama, but I still get the drama and I laughed.

Are we happy with this decision? She said.

Extremely. I said.

Ok. We will revisit this later to see if we have grown any feelings towards them in the next few weeks because sex can complicate things. She responded.

This year is about me. I need to date and enjoy different adventures without having to answer to someone. I said.

AND I DID JUST THAT!

Tatyaniah, I know you must get to the bank before it closes so we will wrap up here today. I will see you next week and we are going to discuss depression and suicide. Please begin to mentally prepare yourself. When I walked out, I felt even better than last week. I was genuinely enjoying this journey of my life.

Tai's Talk

Some reading this may say that what I did is hoe behavior, they would never do that, or that is how you get sexually transmitted diseases and whatever else they can think of. But guess what, we are all entitled to live our lives however we want. I never caught a sexually transmitted disease and I do not regret or feel bad for a thing, I live in my truth. We all do things in our personal lives that someone will not agree with, but so what? Their opinion of you does not matter. The version of you that someone created in their minds DOES NOT MATTER! FUCK THEM!

What is scarier the monsters in your closet?

Or the monsters in your head?

3rd Session

Just as before I pulled in the parking lot, took a deep breath, paid my copay and I waited.

Tatyaniah. She stated.

Hey, how are you? I asked.

Good and yourself? She asked.

I am well. I responded.

Good, because today we are going to dig deep. Pick up the tissues just in case you need them at any point. Today we are allowing ourselves to be vulnerable. I am not judging you. She stated.

Ok. I replied.

Before we start let's recap last week. We recapped. She asked was there anything that happened since we last saw each other that I wanted to talk about.

I saw her again; we went for a walk because she's in a dark place and she said she always felt like I was the most positive person in her life even though she said otherwise at times. Of course, I care about her and I've been sharing some of the things I'm learning here with her. I said anxiously.

I thought you did not want to be friends. She replied.

I do not, but I know how dark her depression gets and I don't want her to do anything drastic.

BOUNDARIES, Tatyaniah. She responded.

I know, we didn't talk much after that besides me asking was she ok. I said.

If we are letting her go, LET HER GO! Stop making excuses to keep her around. She said.

I know, I am working on me. I replied.

Draw me a picture of what you feel and or see when your depression hits. She instructed.

Silence

I colored the paper black and drew a red zigzag line halfway through it and said done.

That was fast. Let us talk about it she said.

Black is for the darkness because I do not know how long I will feel that way and red is for the pain. I spoke.

But it's only halfway through. She said puzzled.

I only halfway allow myself to feel certain things. I responded.

When did the depression start? She asked.

When I was a teenager? I said puzzled.

And what led up to that? She asked.

Homelessness, feeling like my mom was committed to putting her kid's feelings in the background for the men in her life, my dad being in and out of jail and in another state constantly telling lies and not showing up when he said he would, and me having to be a mom before my time. I spoke.

And now? She spoke.

I still harbor some of those resentful feelings, I lost Michael and Dawn to suicide, miscarriage grief, like am I not supposed to be a mom? Feeling alone and like I could be so much farther in life I responded.

She wrote as I spoke.

Have you ever had suicidal thoughts? She asked.

Yes, when I was in middle school. I spoke.

Silence

And why didn't you go through with it? She asked.

What is going to happen to my siblings after I die is one of my biggest fears. I spoke.

And now? She asked.

No. I said.

Your siblings mean the world to you and I can tell by the way that you describe the relationships with all y'all that it's a strong bond and extremely impressive with how blended it is. She stated.

Thanks. I replied.

Describe the homelessness. She stated.

Silence

I was in elementary school, we lived in hotels, we lived with my mom's friends, we spent a lot of time in our blue van, and we spent a lot of time wondering where out next meals were going to come from. We were a family of eight. Nine sometimes. One specific day that I'll never forget is we woke up for school per usual in the hotel. It was a queen suite with two beds a pull-out couch. As everyone got dressed my mom laid in bed, her fiancé at the time was up moving around with us and I was making breakfast the best way I knew how. My brother looked at me and said I am tired of eating toaster strudels. I responded saying shut up, this is what we have. Eat breakfast at school if we have time but stop. He took his plate and walked away. I turned around and said Ma and she said Tai, I heard it. I am trying to get us out of this situation. I finished breakfast, made sure we were ready, and we got in the car and went to school. That day I went to class after dropping my sister off to hers and I felt defeated. I was fighting back tears for a long time because I was mentally exhausted. My teacher would ask was I ok and every time I said yes, and she would keep me busy. After school that day I found a $20 bill on the ground and ran to the van excited to tell everyone and little did I know that the money I found was how we were going to eat that day. We put some in gas and we went to taco bell and got food before heading to the hotel. My mom and her fiancé did what they could. He worked on houses and the winter was off season, so money was not coming in the way it did during the spring and summer and my mom was laid off from her job as a nurse and had to find another one. Do you know what is like to sacrifice being full just to make sure that the younger ones ate enough because they did not really understand the situation? Do you know how strong you must be to deal with all of that at home and still manage to go to school and be on the honor roll and try to be normal and make friends? Once we got out of that situation, we moved into a two bedroom apart. I shared a room with my sister and my uncle. My stepbrother went back to his mom, my mom was back working and so was her fiancé. Things were turning around, but my darkness was not. During this time, I use to wonder why my mom would not leave him, how could she allow us to get to this point? But that was my mother and I stayed. I managed. I tried. While my mom was back working, I had to babysit my siblings and her friend's kids, cook, clean, do my homework and make sure theirs was done and discipline them. I was not even 13. I just wanted to be a kid. I told her.

That is a lot for a child to handle, anyone for that matter. It is honorable the way you stick by your siblings and I understand why you give them everything, but Tatyaniah that is not your job. It was not your job then and it is not your job now. You must realize that what happened then molded you into being the person you are now. Talk to your mom, genuinely tell her how you feel and if you cannot talk about it, write her a letter. But get the feelings out and once you do begin healing and letting them go. You cannot change the past, but you determine the future. She responded.

We sat in silence as she took notes.

Tai's Talk

To the parents that have older children that they make constantly babysit, cook, take care of their younger siblings, and miss out being a kid and enjoying it; they are probably overwhelmed. They probably just want to be a kid that focuses on chores and school. They did not make those kids. Every situation is different, and you may not be able to afford childcare, but allow your kids to be kids so that they don't feel like they had to grow up too soon. Just because your parents did it with you, does not mean it was right.

Who was Michael? She asked.

Silence

WAS... that word was sticking to me at that moment because my emotions were already high, and I cannot believe that I am speaking about him in past tense. Still.

Michael was the only person I vented to growing up. Our mothers are close friends and ultimately, they are my family. When we lived in Virginia my mom's best friends and kids were our family along with our uncle and aunt because no one ever bothered to come visit us unless they lived with us. We only saw them when we traveled to them and I hated that. That is why I feel the way I do now about only seeing my best friend when I travel to her for real. Michael and I talked about everything; he was always telling me facts that I did not care about, but I always listened. Especially about airplanes, that was his thing, which is where he wanted to be in life. We even slept in the same bed and our parents got suspicious once thinking we were more than friends and we NEVER crossed those lines. That was my brother. After we moved away, we did not talk as much which made losing him hurt even worse. Because why wasn't I there for him the way I used to be? I stated.

And what happened? She asked.

He committed suicide, in public. I spoke.

And how did you find out? She asked.

My best friend that lives in Norfolk use to date him. She called me one day and told me that someone told her about an incident at a gun range. I got on Instagram and saw the post and people telling me that they are sorry for my loss because they know how close we were. I called my mom who had just given birth to my youngest sister and his mom and she did not answer. That set the precedence that it was probably true. My mom confirmed it was. I broke down for weeks, because WTF! I would have been there more if I knew. I could not even accept my youngest sister for months because every time I thought about her, I thought about losing him. Harsh, but that was reality to me. I spoke.

And did you go to his funeral? She asked.

He did not have one, but I did not go to the memorial service either. I stated.

Why? She asked.

Because I was not strong enough. I spoke.

Is this hard for you right now? She asked.

Yes. I got this though. I replied.

It's okay to feel weakness and pain right now.

Silence.

Can you tell me about Dawn? She asked.

Dawn was so loud, so obnoxious, and outspoken but she was positive to me. She suffered from bad anxiety and we all knew. Dawn was always in my corner, but she always corrected me if I was wrong. If I were ever on punishment, she would tell my mom that she was coming to get me to help her clean, cook and watch the kids. She is one of my mom's close friends too. Well, was. She made the best cornbread and once I learned how to make it her way, I never made it any other way. I wish she were here a lot of the time. I remember one day in 8th grade I told my mom I wanted to run track and she told me that I was not going to make the team because I was too lazy. Do you know how much words stick to your children? To my mom it was probably another day, but to me that was a day that would forever be embedded in my mind. Dawn came over three times that week to make me run to and from certain points by a certain time. She was the first person I wanted to tell that I made the team. She told me good job, keep going. I knew because of work she could not make my first meet, but I was going to show her that it wasn't for nothing. At my first track meet I placed 1st in all my events, honestly the entire team did. Ruffner Middle School placed first in everything during our first meet. My best friend from Norfolk was there that day and came home with me and my other best friend at the time was on the team too. I was so happy and so eager to rub it in my mom's fact that not only did I make it, but I was good. Dawn congratulated me and motivated me all the time. I needed her around still. She committed a murder suicide a few years ago the day before my youngest sisters' birthday. It hurt to mourn her and still try to celebrate my sister. It is unfair to her that her birthday is surrounded by tragic events. I used to think it was selfish that dawn left us, but I know she was sick and felt like she could not take it anymore. I wish her kids got to experience more life with her. I remember before she passed that her, my mom and another one of my mom's friends took a trip to Las Vegas and she woke me up super early one morning and said "Tai if anything ever happens to me, get this tattoo that says save me, I'm fine" like mine and I laughed it off and said okay, lady and she let me go back to sleep. I promise I am going to find the strength to get it one day. I said.

Have you forgiven her? She asked.

Yes, I just miss her now. I replied.

How does it feel to be able to express these things about the both of them? She asked.

It feels great to be able to talk about them and it fills me. I said.

How do you deal with death? She asked.

I do not. I replied.

Why? She asked.

I have a hard time accepting change, I have a hard time accepting that these people are no longer here, and I want them to be. I responded.

Who else have you lost that really hurt you? She asked.

One of my favorite cousins were killed in 2015 and that broke me the most. I literally was not myself for so long after losing him because I feel like I was taking loss after loss. It still feels strange that he is not here. I have not even deleted his number out of my phone, I am not there yet. I replied.

Grief takes time. Everyone grieves differently. And there is no rush, because grief is just like healing; you can be fine for a long time and then one day something will remind you of them and you are sad. That is normal, but do not let that sadness take over you. Please try to find comfort in the memories you shared with them. She told me.

I try and I genuinely appreciate the way you handle our sessions. I told her.

Let me be honest with you, I think that you know exactly what you need to do in every situation in your life, you just do not do it. You know all the answers and paths you need to take in life, but you need to be more disciplined to get the change that you want. She stated.

I know. I replied.

I want you to write a letter to everyone you've loss, burn it when you are done and start to release any negative emotions you may be suppressing. I am going to see you in two weeks because I do not think you need to see me every week, but you know you can get on the portal and email or call me if you need me.

If you did not want to see me, just say that. I told her.

We both laughed and ended the session.

Tai's Talk

Anxiety and depression are real. You may have friends, family members, team members or coworkers suffering in silence. When you notice changes in people, even if they are small, ask questions or even offer to spend time with them. They may not be ready to open up about their issues, but they will not forget who was there and who was not. And to my black community specifically, stop minimizing your friends and families cry for help by telling them "that's just the devil at work" or "we don't go to therapy we just pray about it and ask the Lord to help us" because prayer is not all that they need. There are crisis counselors, therapist, and other resources available if they need them. We as a community need to understand that going to therapy IS OK.

4th Session

I left work, drove to Columbia, took a deep breath in the parking lot, walked in and paid my copay and waited.

Tatyaniah, are you ready? She asked.

Yes, like girl we need to talk. I said as I laughed.

She laughed and said I am dying to hear it.

Well let's start with the two psychopaths I call ex's. I said.

They're psychopaths now? She said as she laughed.

Girl, yes. Because let me tell you what he did, he saw that I was at her house one day because she called me after getting sloppy drunk and she needed me to come get her. She does not have any family that lives here and very few people she calls friends so of course I went. I took her in her apartment and took care of her from that night and up until the next afternoon. When I got home that day there was a note in my door that said, "I saw you with her." At first, I was nervous after I read it, so I cocked my gun and cleared my house the way the Army taught me before sitting at my desk. I realized it was his handwriting and I called and cussed him out because why are you doing creepy stuff like that. Why are you so concerned about what I am doing, and I know the females you are out going away with, like sir go to hell for real! He was yelling that I lied about being done with her and he drove to her apartment complex when he saw that I wasn't home because I didn't answer, and he knew why. And I am just like sir, friends DO NOT DO THIS. And his response was I DO NOT GIVE A FUCK! He has never liked my relationship with her because it took me away from him. I tried to explain the situation to him even though I did not owe him that, but it did not matter, he didn't want to hear any of it. I expressed to her.

Tai's Talk

Once you realize that NO ONE owes you anything, life will get better for you. Your parents once you are grown, significant other, siblings, and friends are not obligated to do anything for you, and they owe you nothing. YOU OWE YOURSELF EVERYTHING! Take accountability.

Therefore, if you wanted to be friend's ma'am, you should not have been having sex with him. Lines got crossed. He misses you and only wants you to himself. She told me.

I see that now. I replied.

Are you really trying to let her go?

Yes. But I cannot just leave her with no one here. I replied.

She did it to you. She responded.

Silence

You must stand on your boundaries. Discipline. Discipline and more discipline please! I know it will not happen overnight.

I know, I felt like I was relapsing, and I have not seen her outside of the building we work in since. And I'm also tired of hearing about how her new boo feels like I'm coming in between them, but really it was the other way around. And I do not even want her anymore. I spoke.

How do you know that? She asked.

Because when I see her, I no longer feel anything. I no longer care if I do not hear from her and I got rid of everything that had sentimental value that she gave me. I replied.

Small steps, I will take it. She spoke.

Thank you. I said with a big smile.

Now, today were digging deep again. Today we are going to discuss the miscarriages. She stated.

Ok, let's do this. I spoke as I took a deep breath.

Do you know why you keep having miscarriages? She asked.

Yes, I have polycystic ovarian syndrome (PCOS). I told her.

So, you know that the miscarriages are out of your control? She asked.

I stared at her.

Yes, I know that. I told her.

So, you know that you should not blame yourself, because medicine and science have no cure for this, right. She replied.

Yes. I spoke.

So, what is it about them that brings you so much pain? She asked.

The loss of life. The excitement of feeling and knowing that life is growing inside me, noticing the changes of my body and then nothing. I have nothing to show for it but scars. I replied.

You are not alone Tatyaniah. She spoke.

Yeah, but I feel like it. Nobody felt that pain but me. I spoke.

Which is true, but to get through this you must find different ways that you possibly may be able to carry a child to term and even if you cannot there are other alternatives. She told me.

I have done my research; I try not to carry that pain so deeply. I am never going to forget them, but I am finding ways to live my life without feeling sorry for myself in that area. I told her.

Grieve however you want; I just want you to fully grasp the fact that this is out of your control. She stated.

I got it; I have been dealing with this for some years now. I know that even if I must adopt, I will be a mother one day. I stated.

There is honestly nothing that I can do to get you through this, I can listen to as much as you are willing to share and remind you of the ways to stay out of your dark place. She responded.

I get that, usually when something triggers me about it, I call or go see him and cry and or talk about it and he listens, holds me, and reminds me that one day we will make it happen and he is willing to be there every step of the way. I told her.

Tell me how you found out you had PCOS. She spoke.

When I was 16, I woke up crying one night because I was suffering from severe abdominal pain. I called my mom crying although she was in the next room, because I could not stand up, let alone walk. She rushed me to Children's Hospital of Kings Daughters (CHKD) in Norfolk, VA. Doctors and nurses spent countless hours running test, asking questions, and guessing in my opinion. They inserted catheters, Pap meres, gave my enemas, CT scans, the whole 9 yards. Only to conclude that I suffer from polycystic ovarian syndrome (PCOS). A cyst burst on one of my ovaries that night which led to the extensive amount of pain I was enduring. But that night changed my life forever. From that day forward I have encountered countless doctors' appointments, ultrasounds, painful menstrual cycles, a series of cyst bursting and four miscarriages. There is no cure for PCOS, only knowledge and different preventative methods. At the age of 16 that is a lot to wrap your head around. I told her.

Did you worry about whether you could have kids starting at that point? She asked.

Yes, honestly. I replied.

Can you describe what PCOS is to me from what you have been through and what you have learned? She asked.

Polycystic ovarian syndrome is a hormone disorder that causes cyst on enlarged ovaries that is presented in 1 in 10 women. 1 in 10. There is no exact cause of this disorder, but it is speculated to be a combination of environmental factors and genetics. PCOS could include symptoms such as acne, hormonal imbalance, menstrual irregularity obesity and excess hair growth to name a few. This disorder can also be linked to infertility, depression, loss of scalp hair and diabetes. Treatments for PCOS include birth control, physical exercise, and medication to prevent/control diabetes. If you have a mother, sister, aunt, or grandmother that has this disorder than you have a greater risk of having it as well. The disorder usually presents itself during the childbearing age after puberty. Adverse health issues that many do not realize are linked to PCOS is high blood pressure, low sexual satisfaction, sleep apnea, cholesterol issues, and endometrial cancer. I told her.

You memorized this information? She asked.

I live this information. I responded.

And how much of PCOS do you suffer from? She asked.

I suffer from menstrual irregularity which included months without a menstrual cycle, extremely pain cycles that have lasted for up to 16 days, acne, depression, excess hair and unlike a majority that worry about excessive weight gain, I struggle gaining and maintaining weight. I suffer from having multiple cysts on both ovaries that have even reached a massive size preventing me from walking. I have had the surgery that removes them from your ovaries, but of course we all know that they come back. I expressed to her.

If you could tell women about PCOS and your journey with it, what would you say to them? She asked.

You want to know what it feels like to die and still be alive? Witness life growing inside you and lose it.

Silence

Most people do not know that PCOS has been linked with depression. I have given birth control a chance, but when I decided that I wanted children and got off it, I felt powerless and defeated because I couldn't get pregnant for the longest timeframe and once, I got pregnant, I was never able to carry to term. Being a mother is drilled into a part of woman hood, so often women that I have spoken to begin to feel like less of a woman once repeated failure begins to set in. I know I did. One thing that we as women must understand that are feeling this way is that this is not our fault. We cannot control what is happening to us. We have other options. We can try IVF if we are not producing results on our own, and yes IVF is expensive, adoption, and surrogacy. We also cannot immediately blame ourselves for not being able to produce because it could be an issue on both ends. Make sure your partners sperm is tested as well. I spoke.

Would you be willing to describe your miscarriage experiences with them and me? She asked.

Sure. I will share with anyone because I want them to know they are not alone. Miscarriages are so common. I spoke.

So why can't you fully understand that? She asked.

I stared at her.

I have had four miscarriages I told her and each one was different.

1. The first time I was 18, and I knew it happened, I felt the pain, I saw the blood and it hurt briefly and then I was able to keep going.

2. The second time I was 21, I was excited, I saw all the changes in my body, I was growing an attachment, we were ready to meet our baby boy or girl. And then it took a turn for the worse, it became painful, at one ultrasound visit I heard your heartbeat and the next it was undetected. I was crushed, because it did not happen naturally, they had to take you out. And he was not there, he was at work, but my sister drove me to the hospital and sat with me, she took me home and stayed until he got home. I am forever grateful for her being the last face before I fell asleep and the first one when I woke up. But I could not sleep, the doctors told me to rest but that day and I was up, moving around, cooking dinner, everything, I couldn't face it. And on top of that, I had just lost one of my favorite uncles and honestly, I was numb. Later I finally broke down and he hugged me while I cried and then I started grieving. Then I started feeling like I was not good enough to be a mother. Then I was drowning in depression. I felt helpless. To have people constantly asking you about the baby, having to repeatedly say I lost them over and over and over again was unbearable.

3. The third time was only three months after the second, I was determined to get pregnant again and it was excited to send him a picture like look we did it. Only to finally get an appointment and there was no baby. It was deemed a chemical pregnancy. Another loss after not even healing from the previous one. IT WAS DARK!!!

4. I really try not to feel the last one, I took that one on the chin, like here we are again. I told her.

And how would you describe yourself after them? She asked.

I was drowning, and I felt like I would never come up for air and no one around me knew because I hid it so well. I did not talk about it, I cried to myself at night, I swallowed all pain. It broke me to see pregnant women thriving while I could not make that happen. It was not jealousy or envy but pain. I have never wished anyone would lose their child, I have supported every friend and family member throughout their pregnancies and never mentioned how that part of me was still broken. I would never take joy away from someone else because I think motherhood is beautiful. I have had countless conversations with women after miscarriages trying to encourage them and lift their spirits because I know that path can become undoubtedly dark. The darker it gets the harder it is to come out. I have experienced days and weeks of not going to work because I was so broken that mentally I could not force myself to move, I could not force myself to talk to anyone, I could not escape the pain. And no one noticed just how far gone I was, not even the man that slept next to me at night. I remember the first time I tried to express how depressed I was to him his response was "you hell" meaning you're tripping and walked away. I was living in my darkest times and he was not there for me physically, mentally, or emotionally, but he was physically in bed with other women. He was slowly killing me even more, but he was too selfish to even see it. He knew he was a reason that the first two times I was so stressed out and my body could not handle it and all the stress was coming from him. He did not care, so why should I? The bad started outweighing the good and it was time for me to go after miscarriage number three. I could not shake that one. A month later, I moved back to Atlanta with my mom. My body was still reacting as if I was pregnant, especially the lactation process and feeling like I was carrying bricks on my chest because the milk was drying up. The pain began to get easier with time. I still have moments of weakness where the smallest trigger about the pain I felt will make my cry for hours, but that does not mean that I am not still healing. Healing is weird honestly; you can be doing great for months and then one day something happens, and those feelings hit you like a ton of bricks. And that is simply fine, just do not let them keep you down. I expressed.

And you somehow still love him through all of this? Through your darkest times. She stated.

I feel like him and I handled our pain differently. I know I could not have been the easiest person to deal with and I was completely detached from life during those times and honestly, I do not think that he was mature enough to be strong enough for the both of us. I spoke.

You must hold him accountable for his actions. She reminded me.

I do. Why do you think we ended up where we did? We just could not recover from everything and I accepted that. I told her.

Do you believe that he is or will change? She asked.

I already see it; he just still has some growing to do. I replied.

What would you personally recommend to any woman that is trying to deal with miscarriages? She asked.

To those struggling with miscarriages and the painful thoughts that you may never have kids due to this here are some things that help me.

- Light a candle!
- Stop watching shows that make you emotional!
- Find a hobby that interest you and stick with it.
- Travel

- Work on your bucket list

- Get a journal and write out your feelings!

- Scream

- Exercise

- Open the blinds to let in sunlight, open a window to let in fresh air and move.

This can become strenuous to couples and so many couples do not make it out. Husbands leave their wives because they cannot conceive, and they really want to be fathers. In my opinion it takes a strong couple to weather this storm. It is okay to feel hurt or betrayed if they leave, those are your feelings. But do not feel defeated. Do not give up. Fight. Every day wake up and fight. Even if waking up is all you did that day, you survived and that may not feel like much, but it is an accomplishment. Crawl, walk, run.

Did this help you? She asked.

Yes, eventually. I told her.

Now that you have told me the main factors in your life that bring you darkness over these last four session, let's talk about how to rebuild yourself. She stated.

Rebuild what exactly? I asked.

Your confidence, your trust, your joy, your mindset. She stated.

Are you confident? Yes, I have never been more confident in my life. I told her.

And your trust? She asked.

Shattered. I do not trust anyone right away, trust is earned. Everyone is given the benefit of the doubt, until they show me, they can or cannot be trusted. I told her.

What brings you joy? She asked.

Baking, marine life, sitting by the water, planning, traveling, zip lining, cooking sometimes, shopping, and learning about different cultures. I replied.

How do you change your thought process and become more open to other perspectives and realize that you are not always right? She asked.

I stared at her.

I must learn to listen with an open heart and mind. I told her.

And when you start to stray away from those things what is going to bring you back? She asked.

I have a dry erase board in my office area that reminds me of different things I have learned here and my goals of the year. I told her.

And we will keep meditating? She asked.

Of course, it really brings me peace. It genuinely helps me. I told her.

I think we need to find some words of affirmation for when you are feeling down. So that you can remember who you are. She spoke.

And what do you have in mind? I asked.

As we wrapped up our session, she told me that she would find an exercise that would be beneficial. She also told me that we are only going to be seeing each other once a month from now on because she feels that I need to practice discipline and trusting myself. I left that session feeling a little bit lighter once again.

Exercise

1. What are a few flaws that you want to fix about yourself?

2. Why do those imperfections bother you?

3. What can you do to fix those imperfections?

4. What are some positive words of affirmation that you can use as a reminder to yourself?

If I was able to do anything while writing this book, I hope I was able to help someone realize that there are many people that have fought battles like ones you may try to suppress. Suppression is not going to work. At some point in life everyone needs to face their past/ trauma because you cannot run away from it forever. Life has a funny way of making things come around full circle. This is how I hope to reach someone, even if it just one person. As previously stated, I am not a counselor, but I am in school working towards being one. And to anyone feeling as if it's too late to go to school, it's not. Do things when you're ready and do not compare yourself to someone else. Comparison can be the thief of joy, especially with millennials and generation Z. Everything that you idolize on social media is not the full picture. To anyone that wants an outlet or someone to vent to whether it be anonymously or not, here are my social media pages dedicated to this journey:

Tiktok: Taystalk

Instagram: Tatyaniah

YouTube: Tay's Talk

www.ingramcontent.com/pod-product-compliance
Lightning Source LLC
Chambersburg PA
CBHW080602090426
42735CB00016B/3320